# Amazing Animal Skills

# SPITS AND SQUIRTS

## HOW ANIMALS SQUIRT TO SURVIVE

## ROBIN KOONTZ

Marshall Cavendish
Benchmark
New York

Special thanks to Donald E. Moore III, associate director of animal care at the Smithsonian Institution's National Zoo, for his expert reading of this manuscript.

Other Marshall Cavendish Offices:  Marshall Cavendish International (Asia) Private Limited, 1 New Industrial Road, Singapore 536196 • Marshall Cavendish International (Thailand) Co Ltd. 253 Asoke, 12th Flr, Sukhumvit 21 Road, Klongtoey Nua, Wattana, Bangkok 10110, Thailand • Marshall Cavendish (Malaysia) Sdn Bhd, Times Subang, Lot 46, Subang Hi-Tech Industrial Park, Batu Tiga, 40000 Shah Alam, Selangor Darul Ehsan, Malaysia

Marshall Cavendish is a trademark of Times Publishing Limited

All websites were available and accurate when this book was sent to press.

Library of Congress Cataloging-in-Publication Data
Koontz, Robin Michal.
Spits and squirts : how animals squirt to survive / by Robin Koontz.
p. cm. — (Amazing animal skills)
Includes index.
Summary: "An exploration of animals who use special skills, such as spitting and squirting, in order to survive"—Provided by publisher.
ISBN 978-0-7614-4909-6 (print)   ISBN 978-1-60870-602-0 (ebook)
1. Saliva—Juvenile literature. 2. Animal defenses—Juvenile literature.
I. Title.
QP191.K66 2012
612.3´13—dc22
2010016863

EDITOR: Joy Bean   PUBLISHER: Michelle Bisson
ART DIRECTOR: Anahid Hamparian   SERIES DESIGNER: Kristen Branch

Photo research by Joan Meisel
Cover photo:  Kim Taylor/Minden Pictures
The photographs in this book are used by permission and through the courtesy of:  *Alamy*: Chuck Carlton, 5; Wildlife Gmbh, 10; Chris Howes/Wild Places Photography, 15(b); Peter Arnold, Inc., 24; imagebroker, 27; Reinhard Dirscherl, 29; Rolf Nussbaumer Photography, 36; fotoNatura, 39. *Corbis*: Barry Lewis/In Pictures, 4. *Getty*: Carole Drake, 8; Michael Fogden, 12; De Agostini, 41. *Minden Pictures*: Doug Perrine, 14; Fred Bavendam, 28; Satoshi Kuribayashi, 32. *Peter Arnold Images*: A. Skonieczny/Arco Images, 1, 2, 7; Gerard Soury/Biosphoto, 18; Daniel Heuclin/Biosphoto, 19. *Photo Researchers, Inc.*: Fletcher & Baylis, 15(tr); Science Source, 37(b). *SuperStock*: Hal Beral VWPics, 16; age fotostock, 21, 22, 23; All Canada Photos, 33; James Urbach, 34; NaturePL, 37(t).

Printed in Malaysia (T)
1 3 5 6 4 2

# CONTENTS

# CHAPTER ONE

# SPIT TO THE RESCUE!

A big gob of spit is pretty gross. It is made up of saliva and whatever else might be hanging out in the mouth, such as snotty mucus or bits of food. Spit and spew can be gummy, gooey, or even frothy, depending on what's in it. So what good is spit other than being slimy and disgusting? In the animal world, spit can come in handy.

Some dogs always have a lot of slobbery saliva coming out of their mouths. That's just how their mouths work.

# HELPFUL SPIT

Spit helps humans and animals eat by making food wet and easy to swallow. Spit also breaks down fat and starch in food. That makes food easier to digest. Spit helps clean our teeth by keeping bacteria from sticking to them. It can also help us taste food before we swallow it. Spit is made up of mostly water, but it has a lot of other stuff, such as DNA, in it. DNA, or deoxyribonucleic acid, contains instructions for everything our cells do.

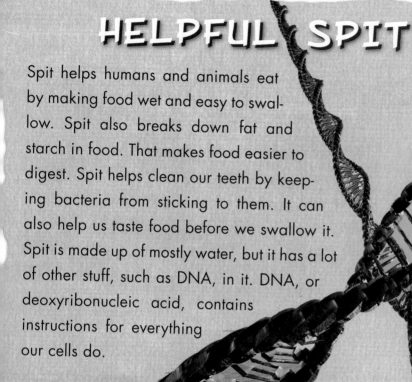

Strands of DNA look like twisted ladders.

Have you ever gone swimming in a pond or river and come out with slimy, sluglike critters attached to your body? Those are bloodsucking leeches, which are found in waters all over the world. Leeches have a special kind of spit that allows them to bite you without you feeling it.

An adult leech sucks the blood of mammals by attaching itself with the suckers it has on the bottom

You may not feel it when you have a leech stuck on you because of the special chemicals leeches have in their spit.

of its body and biting through the skin. It spits out stuff that makes the skin numb, so the host feels no pain. While the leech feeds on blood, it can grow up to ten times its normal size. Yikes!

Leech spit might sound gross, but it can be a good thing. Leeches are popular with doctors because there is a special chemical in their spit that keeps blood from clotting. Doctors have discovered that some leech spit can help people with bad injuries heal faster. Doctors who use leeches attach them

6

to patients to keep blood flowing after surgeries such as limb transplants.

Spit is useful for a lot of reasons. Some animals use it to attract mates. The male scorpion fly gives a glob of spit to his mate to show he cares. The male spits onto a leaf in the woods where he lives. Soon the spit glob hardens into a tasty snack for the female scorpion fly. Yuck! But to a female scorpion fly, that spit treat is as yummy as a box of chocolates.

Scorpion flies get their name because the male has a tail that looks like a scorpion's stinging tail. But instead of a stinger, the tip of the male scorpion fly's tail has a pair of claspers he can use to grab a female. He makes sure to offer her that hardened glob of spit just in case

Not all that long ago, barbers did a lot more than cut hair. They were also a town's dentist and doctor. They used leeches to treat their patients for all kinds of ailments. People believed that **bloodletting** would help cure indigestion, tetanus, asthma, and other medical problems.

A male scorpion fly has handy claspers at the end of his tail.

7

## MEDICINAL SPIT

Kodiak bears in Alaska chew up the root of a plant called Ligusticum and spit the sloppy goop on their paws. Then they rub the goop into their fur. A legend says that the bear taught American Indians that the root was a good medicine for healing wounds. This plant's common name is bear medicine or bear root.

the female doesn't want to be grabbed.

A vinegaroon is a kind of whip scorpion that lives in tropical and subtropical areas. It does not have good eyesight and relies on feeling vibrations through the ground to know if prey is nearby. It has an interesting special defense: it squirts a vinegar-like mist if it is upset. The mist from the vinegaroon contains mostly acetic acid, which is the main ingredient in vinegar. When animals are hit with this mist, they will run away.

Animals of all kinds use spit and other body fluids to hide in, to protect their

Some vinegaroons can be more than 6 inches (15 centimeters) long.

babies, or as weapons to use against enemies. Many animals even use spit to catch a meal! Animals that spit, squirt, or spew their juices may seem gross, but all that sticky stuff helps them to survive.

# CHAPTER TWO

# HOME SWEET SPIT HOME

One way animals use spit is to create a cozy, safe place to live. Have you ever walked through a meadow and noticed a lot of foamy spit in the grass? It looks like somebody went on a spitting spree! If you looked closely, you might even have spotted a few little bugs trapped inside the spit. The bugs aren't really trapped. You were looking at a baby insect called a frog-hopper in its house. The frothy mess is sometimes called frog spit. An adult frog-hopper lays eggs on the grass at summer's end. The eggs

Baby frog hoppers stay safe by creating a fluid that looks like spit. The goo protects them from the elements.

hatch the following spring. A baby, called a nymph, whips up a mass of froth from a gland in its body. The spit is made of fluid from its gut, along with a substance similar to mucus. The nymph releases air bubbles along with the gooey spit. The bubbly house is very strong in wind or rain. The nymph stays safely inside and chomps on the grass, usually undisturbed.

Frogs also use a spitlike substance in an interesting way. The Tungara frog from Central and South America makes a house of bubbles to protect its babies. The male frog hangs out in a shallow pool of water and sings for a mate. When he finds his truelove, she picks him up and carries him to a special spot she has chosen for their nursery. The female squirts a mess of eggs and jelly. The helpful male collects the gunk with his hind feet and whips it up into a foamy

Tungara frogs use teamwork to protect their eggs.

mass as big as a fist. The eggs hatch within two days, and the frog babies, called tadpoles, swim away.

Siamese fighting fish, which can be found in Southeast Asia, also create a nest of bubbles for babies. The male fish blows spit-coated bubbles. The bubbles mass together on the water's surface. He places eggs into the bubbles and guards the spit nest until the babies hatch about two days later.

## INTERIOR NURSERIES

Keeping babies safe while they grow up is a top priority for many animals. Spit and other body fluids can make a safe haven for youngsters.

Darwin frog dads go to extreme lengths to make sure their babies stay safe.

How would you like to grow up inside your dad's throat? Some frogs do just that. The female Darwin's frog from South America lays her eggs in wet mud. The male frog watches over the eggs. When he thinks the eggs are about to hatch, he gathers them up one by one and stuffs them into the expandable vocal sacs in his throat. The eggs hatch in there, and the tadpoles soon turn into frogs. In about two weeks, when the baby frogs are ready for the world, the dad spits them out.

The gastric brooding frog from Australia goes one better. The mother frog swallows her eggs and lets her babies hatch in her stomach. Poor mom can't eat for up to eight weeks while the baby tadpoles grow up and later become little frogs. When they are old enough to be out on their own, they crawl into mom's throat and spill out of her mouth.

Gastric brooding frog moms go without food until their babies leave her belly nursery.

13

## HANDY SPIT HIDEAWAYS

A tube of spitlike mucus makes a nice home for an undersea peacock worm. The worm mixes its mucus with sand and mud, constructing a long, skinny tube that sticks up from the seafloor. It hides inside and sticks out its feathery tentacles to snag plankton, its favorite food.

When the ocean-dwelling Bleeker's parrot fish wants to sleep, it uses special glands to spit out a sleeping bag made of mucus. The slimy cocoon protects the fish from enemies. They think the hidden parrot fish is just another ball of slime.

How about a house of spit that you can eat? The Indian edible-nest swiftlet is a small, brown

This fish, called a Bleeker's parrot fish, hides in what looks like a slimy sleeping bag.

bird that usually lives in caves. The male spits out a long, jellylike strand of rubbery spit from salivary glands under his tongue. He winds up the goo into a bowl-shaped nest and glues it to the cave or cliff wall. The spit nest hardens, and he and his mate raise their babies in it. One cave can house thousands of swiftlet nests.

Swiftlets' nests are the main ingredient in bird's nest soup, which is a Chinese delicacy. The nests are mixed with chicken, spices, and other flavors and cooked. It is a favorite food in China and Hong Kong.

These hardened nests made by birds called swiftlets are used in a soup recipe that is popular in China.

# Clothes Made of Spit!

Silkworms from China spin a spit cocoon from one strand of silk that can be almost a mile long. People unwind the silk and use it to make silk thread and fabric.

# CHAPTER THREE

# EAT SPIT!

Many animals offer already-digested food to their babies in the form of spit-up. Pelicans live just about everywhere there are fish, especially near oceans. The pelican has a long bill with a large throat pouch attached to it. It uses the pouch as a net to catch fish. Once a baby pelican hatches, the parents' pouches become bowls. When a white pelican feeds its babies, it spits up the fish it gobbled earlier into the pouch. The baby gets a nice bowl of fish-spit soup!

Pelicans have built-in bowls from which they feed their babies.

The pigeon is another type of bird found almost worldwide that spits up for its babies. Most birds, including the pigeon, have a storage place in the chest called a crop. The crop can store and soften food before a bird digests it or spews it for its babies. Pigeons also produce a milklike substance in their crops that is very good for baby pigeons. Both parents spit up milk for their babies for more than two weeks, after which the babies start to eat more solid food.

Owls do not have crops, so everything they eat goes right to their stomachs. Part of the owl stomach, called the gizzard, is like a

CROP

Pigeons and other birds store food in a crop.

**Fast Fact**

Baby pigeons are called squabs.

17

filter. It collects the stuff an owl can't digest, such as the bones, fur, teeth, and feathers of its prey. The gizzard compresses it into a pellet, and eventually the owl stretches its neck, opens its beak, and—*erp!*—spits up the pellet. Animals such as mice and rabbits eat these spit-up leftovers. Yum!

Owl pellets can look like dried up poop.

## SHARE AND SHARE ALIKE

Some babies encourage mom or dad to spit up for them. When they are hungry, woodland wolf pups sniff and lick at a parent's mouth until he or

Hungry wolf pups will encourage mom or dad to share any food they may have in their bellies.

she spits up digested food for them. Wolf moms and other family members also get to share in the feast. The nice, warm spit-up is a healthy supplement to the fresh food the wolves bring home.

Vampire bats of Central and South America also share spit-up meals with their family and friends. To eat, they make a small incision with their teeth in their blood host, such as a cow, and lap up the blood that flows from the tiny wound. Like leeches, vampire bats have a special ingredient in their spit that keeps the blood from clotting. A bat that finds a nice meal returns to its night **roost** and spits up blood to share with those who weren't successful at finding dinner that night. This rare mutual buddy system creates special bonds among the group members.

A vampire bat can walk, run, or hop along the ground to stalk its prey.

# CHAPTER FOUR

# SPIT UP FOR YOUR FOOD

When a housefly lands on food it wants to eat, it spits on it. The spit contains an enzyme called volidrop that helps to predigest the food. The spit mixture melts a tiny spot on the food. The fly then sucks up the spit and the melted meal. Then it might spit it out and suck it up again. Flies eat a wide variety of things. They enjoy eating rotting, disease-ridden garbage as much as they love your bologna sandwich. A fly can have millions of nasty bacteria in its gut

A fly sucks up its own spit to get a meal.

## Nosey Feet

Flies have most of their taste and smell sensors on their leg hairs. That's why flies rub their legs together so often. They're checking to see how yummy your sandwich will taste!

and swarming over its legs and body. This means a fly can deposit bacteria every time it lands and spits up.

But not all fly spit is bad for us. Scientists have discovered that although the proteins in black fly spit help the fly to spread disease, those proteins can be used to make vaccines that prevent the same diseases.

The freshwater soft-shell clam is also called a squirt clam for a good reason. It burrows in sand or mud as deep as twice its shell size. It sticks up two tubes called siphons. It uses one siphon to suck in water and

Sometimes you can see a clam's siphon on the sand's surface. That means you may run across something just like this on the beach.

food bits. Gills trap the food while the other siphon expels the filtered water. Soft-shell clams can filter 1 quart (0.9 liters) of water an hour. The only signs the clams are around are the little siphon holes in the mud and sand. But if you walk close and disturb one, the clam will squirt water from its hole. This is how clam diggers find the clams.

A sea star lives in shallow parts of the ocean and is a master at spitting up. It doesn't move very fast, but neither do the clams it likes to eat. The star puts its mouth on the seam between the

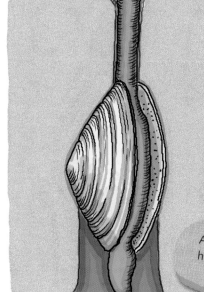

A clam's body is usually hidden away below the surface of the sand.

clamshells and pulls them apart with its strong arms covered in suckers. Once the clam opens up, the star spits its stomach inside. Then it digests the clam's soft body parts. When it is full, the star sucks its stomach back in through its mouth.

The ocean-dwelling sea cucumber can spew up more than its stomach. The sea cucumber gets its name because its soft, elongated body, covered in warty bumps, looks like a cucumber. Many

This sea cucumber is expelling its inner organs in order to protect itself.

varieties can produce a toxin that is deadly to small animals and fish but not to humans. When a sea cucumber feels it is about to be eaten, it can spew all of its internal organs. While the predator feasts on the guts, the sea cucumber just crawls away and eventually grows new organs.

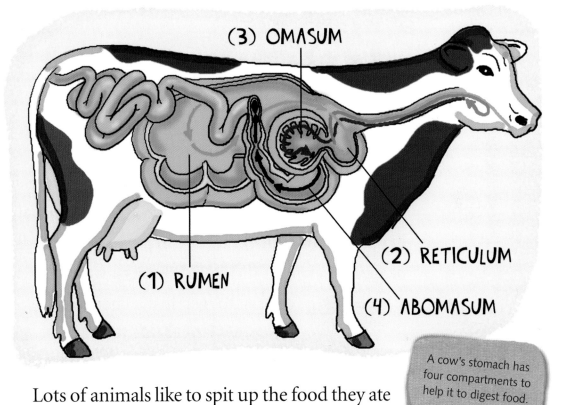

(3) OMASUM

(2) RETICULUM

(1) RUMEN

(4) ABOMASUM

A cow's stomach has four compartments to help it to digest food.

Lots of animals like to spit up the food they ate earlier and eat it again. Cows, goats, camels, and other **ruminants** don't chew their food. They swallow grass and other vegetation in hunks and then let **microorganisms** in their stomach break it down for them. Hours later, they hack it up into their mouths and mix the soft, gooey mass, called cud or bolus, with spit. And then they swallow it again!

Fast Fact

The term "chewing the cud" means meditating or pondering.

# CHAPTER FIVE

# SPIT FOR DEFENSE

R uminant cud can be a spit-full defense! Camels, llamas, alpacas, and other animals in the camelid family that live in plains, grasslands, or deserts around the world spit as a warning for others to get lost. Their spit is a nasty wad of three stomach compartments' worth of green goo. They usually spit if they feel upset or threatened. Luckily, they rarely spit at people. Huge birds called vultures eat

Camel spit is like spit-up, so stand back if you see a camel looking angry.

26

dead stuff. That's their job. If it feels threatened, a vulture will vomit foul-smelling, partially digested meat on or near its attacker. The putrid mix of spit and rotting meat is so nasty, it can sting if the intruder is close enough to get it in the face or eyes. It is no wonder that vultures don't have many enemies.

Sometimes a vulture eats so much, it becomes too full to fly. So just before takeoff, it spits up a bunch of undigested food. Then other animals come along and eat the vomit. What a nice way to share a meal!

Not everyone waits for vultures to share the feast on their own terms. The bald eagle, our nation's emblem, eats vulture vomit. Bald eagles seek out vultures and bother them to make them feel threatened.

Vultures are probably most well-known for eating dead animals.

This makes the vultures vomit, and the bald eagles then enjoy a putrid feast.

## SEA SPITTERS

There are a lot of spewers and spitters in the sea. An octopus has its own special way to confuse its enemies, such as eels, dolphins, and sharks. It squirts a cloud of black ink into the water that looks like a smoke screen. Then it can suck water into its body and shoot it out of a special tube, helping it to make a jet-powered getaway.

## Spitting Image

The squid is an especially creative spitter. It can spit out a dense blob of ink called a pseudomorph. The ink forms a squidlike shape that holds the attacker's attention while the squid turns pale and jets away.

Another sea creature uses the same trick as the squid and octopus, only its ink causes a powerful and strange chemical reaction. The sea hare is a kind of sea slug that is shaped like a rabbit or hare. It has thin shell plates that cover just its heart and gills. It moves slowly like a slug, not quickly like a hare.

When an enemy such as a spiny lobster threatens a sea hare, the sea hare releases a cloud of ink along with a snotty secretion called opaline. Scientists found that the opaline contains stuff that upsets the lobster's nervous system. When a lobster is exposed to the secretion, it thinks the cloud of chemicals is food and tries to eat it instead of the sea hare.

Fast Fact

In some countries and cultures, squid ink is a popular food. The ink is gathered from squid and either packaged or sold fresh.

A sea hare relies on a defensive spray to protect it from harm.

The hagfish is sometimes called the most disgusting creature in the sea. Its body is covered with glands that excrete a sticky slime. It can surround itself and an enemy with a huge, gooey mess. Then it ties itself into a knot to wipe the slime away and make an escape.

Tiny sea creatures called ostracods create an underwater light show in the dark. They shoot chemicals from built-in nozzles that mix with water

A hagfish will excrete slime if it feels threatened.

Fast Fact

Wood ants sometimes work together to squirt jets of formic acid that can reach several inches above their nest.

to produce blue puffs of light. A male trying to attract a mate swims quickly through the water, leaving trails of pretty blue lights behind it.

## LITTLE LAND SQUIRTERS

Some small land creatures are also excellent squirters. Termites are related to cockroaches and grasshoppers and are found throughout the world. They live in colonies with a queen, workers, and soldiers. Some soldiers have hornlike nozzles on their heads. They can squirt a nasty liquid through the nozzles to scare off enemies.

The African bombardier beetle is one of the most amazing squirters in

### Bodyguards

Some termite soldiers guard the colony with their bodies. If the nest is invaded, they blow themselves up like balloons to block the entry tunnels. When the attackers get close, the soldiers explode, plastering the enemies with their gooey termite guts. This exploding is called autothysis.

31

A bombardier beetle can squirt enemies with a high-pressure jet stream of nasty stuff.

## POWER IN NUMBERS

Wood ants will sometimes work together to squirt jets of formic acid that can reach several inches above their nest.

the insect world. This creature is a super sharpshooter. It can raise its rear end, aim, and fire a boiling mix of chemicals in any direction. Now that's some serious bug spray!

This horned lizard is relaxed. But watch out if it feels threatened because it will grow much larger.

The North American horned lizard, also called the horny toad, can really freak out a potential attacker. If an enemy such as a snake or a bird gives it any grief, it will puff up to twice its size and lunge at its attacker. It might also vibrate its tail and hiss. But most amazing of all, some horned lizards can shoot long streams of blood from their eyes as far as several feet. They can spray blood forward or backward using one or both eyes. This disgusting act usually turns off any attacker.

# CHAPTER SIX

# TOXIC SPIT

Most spit and spew is harmless. But some spit can be dangerous to other animals, including humans. The lubber grasshopper, found mostly in the southeastern United States, has a way to warn enemies not to take a bite out of it. It spews a toxic spray from its belly while making a scary hissing noise. It might also spew out a dark glob of digested plants with more toxins. If an enemy doesn't get the hint and eats the lubber anyway, it can get sick or even die.

This lubber grasshopper would not make a good snack.

Spitting cobras can spray several feet in front of them.

Poisonous snakes usually have to bite something in order for their venom to come out, but some cobras can also spit at an attacker. One spitting cobra from Mozambique, Africa, uses muscles to squeeze the glands that store its poisonous venom. The venom shoots from spray holes in front of the two fangs. Stand back! The poisonous venom can blind an attacker and cause scarring.

The cane toad likes to live in warm, humid places. It can spray a toxic substance from glands behind its eyes. It turns to face the enemy and then squirts, often killing the attacker!

## Not Welcome Anymore

Cane toads were introduced to Australia to try to control certain crop pests. The toads didn't like to eat the pests, but they ate a lot of other native wildlife. Now the toads are considered an **invasive** species.

## TOUCH ME NOT!

The poison arrow frog has skin secretions so poisonous that just touching one can kill an enemy. People who hunt with blowpipes can rub the tip of a weapon over the frog's back to load the weapon with enough poison to kill an animal.

The puffer fish is almost as poisonous as the poison arrow frog. Its skin, blood, and some organs contain poison that can kill a human. The puffer fish, also called the blowfish, doesn't spit or spew but instead sucks! If it feels threatened, the puffer will inflate itself by sucking in water or air until it is much bigger than normal. If the attacker tries to eat the puffer anyway, its poison will kill the enemy!

Poison arrow frogs are brightly colored as a warning that enemies should keep away.

## DEADLY TO PLANTS

Some spit is poisonous to our food. The Hessian fly is a terrible pest in many countries that grow wheat. One bite from the fly's larva can make a wheat plant droop, topple over, and die. How? With its poisonous spit! For hundreds of years, the fly's larvae have been killing wheat crops with their deadly spit. In recent years, scientists have discovered that they can use the spit to help make wheat plants resist the toxic spew.

A puffer fish looks harmless when it's not threatened (left and center) but looks much more harmful when puffed up (right).

The larvae of Hessian flies can damage wheat crops with their spit.

### Fast Fact

Even though they are deadly poisonous, puffers are a food delicacy in some countries. Chefs must prepare the fish very carefully and only serve the parts of the fish that are poison-free.

37

# CHAPTER SEVEN

# CATCH IT WITH SPIT

Some animals use their spit to catch a meal. How would you like to be trapped by the spit of a creepy, caterpillar-like worm? A walking worm can squirt out a nasty spit trap for its prey. Luckily, these worms are very small and shy.

A walking worm spends its days hiding on the forest floor or in termite tunnels and only comes out at night or during rainy periods. The worm has two bumps near its mouth. When it spots a tasty-looking insect,

## Hard to Find

Walking worms, also called velvet worms or spitting worms, live in forest regions of South America, Africa, the Caribbean, and Oceania. There are about ninety known species, but the worms are rarely seen. Fossils show that marine relatives of walking worms lived 520 million years ago.

Walking worms are able to shoot slime at a possible meal.

it squirts a stream of slime from the bumps. The glue-like slime traps the insect like a net and hardens right away. The insect is captured in a spit cage, and the worm can lunch at its leisure.

Walking worms aren't the only spit trappers. Spitting spiders also have a spit weapon to catch potential meals, and this one is deadly. The spitting spider has a poison gland in its large head. This gland is connected to the spider's silk spinnerets in its rear end.

A spitting spider doesn't hang out on a web waiting for dinner to come to it, like many spiders do. This spider leaves its dark corner in a cave, house, or shed and goes hunting, mostly at night. It roams in the dark and uses its long front legs to detect prey.

A walking worm searches for food, which it will trap with slime.

Once the spitting spider detects a yummy moth, fly, or other possible meal, it sneaks up on it until it is close but not too close. Then the spider squeezes its body to combine poison and silk as it spits out two deadly streams. It sways from side to side and covers the prey in a zigzag pattern. The sticky mess traps, **paralyzes**, and soon kills the prey. Once the prey is dead, the spider releases it from the silk and enjoys a tasty meal.

A spitting spider wraps its prey in a certain way so that it can not get away.

## READY, AIM, FIRE!

Archerfish are among the most amazing hunters of the animal kingdom. The fish live in coastal waters and rivers from East Africa to Australia. The flat body of an archerfish makes it almost invisible

**Fast Fact**

Like flies, spiders can eat only food that is liquid. They either inject digestive fluids into their prey or spit up on it before they can polish it off.

An archerfish looks harmless, but it has a special weapon.

from above. Its black-and-white markings also help to hide it in sun-dappled water. Its large eyes are located close to the mouth, giving it good vision. All an archer needs in order to hunt insects buzzing through the air is a handy water pistol. And that's just what it's got, sort of.

An archerfish uses its tongue and the top of its mouth to make a long, barrel-like groove. It takes careful aim at an unsuspecting insect high

above. Then—*zap!*—it squeezes
its gills to accurately launch squirts
of water up to 4 feet (more than 1
meter) above the water surface. The
insect is knocked out of the sky, and
the archer is there to catch it. If the
archerfish misses on the first try, it
will fire again in rapid succession.

Archers learn to spit when
they are very young. They swim
in hunting parties. Sometimes

Archerfish have very
good aim.

several archers shoot at the same prey. When the prey falls, they all rush to eat it. Party time!

The Australian snubfin dolphin is a newsworthy spitter, too. It was just discovered in 2005 and is considered to be rare. Snubfins have been spotted spitting water at fish they hope to eat. They hunt in groups and fire jets of water from their mouths at a school of fish. The spitting appears to help round up the fish into tightly packed groups so they are easier to catch.

## SURVIVAL SPEW

Lots of animals spit, spray, spew, squirt, and vomit as clever ways to get through the day and night. They use their disgusting abilities for defense, safe housing, and protecting their young. Spit and spew help animals catch food and feed their babies. Some spit even helps them to attract and impress potential mates. Without these handy bodily fluids to help them get along, many of these animals would not be able to survive in the world.

# GLOSSARY

**bloodletting**  the process of removing blood from the body

**clotting**  forming a hardened, dry mass of blood

**enzyme**  a type of protein made by living cells

**gizzard**  a muscular pouch in many birds and reptiles used for grinding food

**habitat**  the type of environment where a living thing flourishes

**host**  one that provides food for another organism

**invasive**  tending to invade, spread, or infringe on something

**microorganism**  any organism that can be seen only with the help of a microscope

**ostracod**  a tiny water creature with a shrimplike body enclosed in a shell

**paralyze**  to make powerless and unable to move

**plankton**  a cluster of small plant and animal organisms floating in freshwater or salt water

**predigest**  to begin the process of digestion

**pseudomorph** a deceptive or irregular form

**putrid** foul or rotten

**roost** a place where winged animals rest or raise young

**ruminant** a hoofed mammal that has a stomach divided into three or four compartments

**saliva** liquid secreted into the mouth by salivary and mucous glands

**secretion** a substance that is released from a gland or cell

**spinneret** an organ that produces threads of silk

**subtropical** relating to regions that border the tropical zone

**vaccine** a preparation used to help increase immunity to a disease

**volidrop** an enzyme secreted by flies

## FIND OUT MORE

### Books

*Animals: A Visual Encyclopedia.* New York: DK Publishing, 2008.

Greenburg, Nicki. *An Octopus Has Deadly Spit* (It's True!). Toronto, Canada: Annick Press, 2007.

*Scholastic Children's Encyclopedia.* New York: Scholastic, 2004.

Uhlenbroek, Charlotte. *Animal Life.* New York, New York: DK Publishing, 2008.

### Websites

Animal Diversity Web
http://animaldiversity.ummz.umich.edu/site/index.html

Animal Planet
http://animal.discovery.com/

National Geographic Kids
http://kids.nationalgeographic.com/

# INDEX

**Pages in boldface are illustrations.**

## ABOUT THE AUTHOR

ROBIN KOONTZ grew up in a wild suburb of Maryland and later lived in West Virginia. She learned from some great people how to respect every living creature. Robin now lives with her husband and various critters in the Coast Range mountains of western Oregon. She shares her office space with spiders and whatever they happen to catch.